Perceval Surname

Ireland: 1600s to 1900s

From Ireland Church Records of Baptism, Marriage and Death

Comprised of Roman Catholic and Church of Ireland Records

From Counties Carlow, Cork, Kerry and Dublin City

Compiled by **Donovan Hurst**

March 5, 2013

ISBN: 1939958059
ISBN-13: 978-1-939958-05-1

Dedication

This work is dedicated to all of those that came before us and shaped our lives to make us the people that we are today.

Table of Contents

Introduction

This is a compilation of individuals who have the surname of Perceval that lived in the country of Ireland from the 1600s to the 1900s. I have placed each entry into one of four categories: Families, Individual Births/Baptisms, Individual Burials, and Individual Marriages. If a marriage entry primarily concerns an Individual Perceval whom is female, then I have placed that entry under the category of Individual Marriages. If a marriage entry primarily concerns an Individual Perceval whom is male, then I have placed that entry under the category of Families. Images of many of these listings are available at http://churchrecords.irishgenealogy.ie/churchrecords/.

To help guide the reader of this work, the format of this book is as follows:

- Main Family Entry (Husband and Wife) (Father and Mother)

  o Child of Main Family Entry, including Spouse(s) when available

    ▪ Grandchild of Main Family Entry, including Spouse(s) when available

      • Great-Grandchild of Main Family Entry, including Spouse(s) when available

(**Bolded Text**) following any entry includes any additional information such as Residence(s), Occupation(s), Signature(s), etc. when available.

Hurst

Some of the fonts used in this work symbolizes Celtic writing. The traditional letters, numbers, and punctuation marks and their Celtic counterparts are as follows:

Traditional Letters (Uppercase & Lowercase)

A a B b C c D d E f G g H h I i J j K k L l M m N n O o P p Q q R r S s T t U u V v W w X x Y y Z z

Celtic Letters (Uppercase & Lowercase)

A a B b C c D ð E e F f G g H h I i J j K k L l M m

N n O o P p Q q R r S s T t U u V v W w X x Y y Z z

Traditional Numbers

1 2 3 4 5 6 7 8 9 10

Celtic Numbers

1 2 3 4 5 6 7 8 9 10

Traditional Punctuation

. , : ' " & - ( )

Celtic Punctuation

. , : ' " & - ( )

Parish Churches

Carlow (Church of Ireland)

Killeshin Parish.

Cork & Ross

(Roman Catholic or RC)

Cork - South Parish and Cork SS. Peter & Paul Parish.

Dublin (Church of Ireland)

Clontarf Parish, Kilmainham Parish, Leeson Park Parish, Rotunda Chapel Parish, St. Anne Parish, St. Audoen Parish, St. Bride Parish, St. Catherine Parish, St. George Parish, St. James Parish, St. John Parish, St. Mark Parish, St. Mary Parish, St. Matthew Parish, St. Michan Parish, St. Nicholas Within Parish, St. Nicholas Without Parish, St. Patrick Parish, St. Paul Parish, St. Peter Parish, St. Stephen Parish, St. Thomas Parish, and St. Werburgh Parish.

Dublin (Roman Catholic or RC)

Rathmines Parish, SS. Michael & John Parish, St. Andrew Parish, St. Catherine Parish, St. James Parish, St. Mary Parish, St. Mary, Haddington Road Parish, St. Mary, Pro Cathedral Parish, St. Michan Parish, and St. Nicholas Parish.

Kerry (Church of Ireland)

Kenmare Parish.

ℱamilies

- Alexander Perceval & Jane L'Estrange – 11 Feb 1808 (Marriage, **St. George Parish**)

Alexander Perceval (husband):

   Residence - St. George Parish & Temple House, Co. Sligo - February 11, 1808

   Occupation - Esquire - February 11, 1808

Jane L'Estrange, daughter of Collin L'Estrange & Grace L'Estrange (daughter-in-law):

   Residence - St. George Parish & Moyston, King's County - February 11, 1808

- Alexander Perceval & Unknown
  - Henry Perceval & Elizabeth Leticia Hutchinson – 10 Jan 1850 (Marriage, **St. Peter Parish**)

Signatures:

Henry Perceval (son):

   Residence - Haddington Terrace, Kingstown - January 10, 1850

   Occupation - Clerk in Holy Orders - January 10, 1850

Elizabeth Leticia Hutchinson, daughter of John Hutchinson (daughter-in-law):

   Residence - 71 Harcourt Street - January 10, 1850

Hurst

John Hutchinson (father):

    Occupation - Barrister at Law

Alexander Perceval (father):

    Occupation - Colonel in Army

Wedding Witnesses:

John Hutchinson & William Hutchinson

Signatures:

- Alexander Bustard Perceval & Emily Douglas – 28 Dec 1842 (Marriage, **St. Mary Parish**)

Signatures:

Alexander Bustard Perceval (husband):

    Residence - 7 Arran Quay, St. Michan Parish - December 28, 1842

Emily Douglas (wife):

    Residence - Capel Street, St. Mary Parish - December 28, 1842

Perceval Surname Ireland: 1600s to 1900s

Wedding Witnesses:

Richard Douglas & William Russell

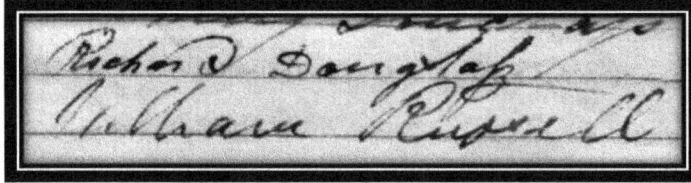

Signatures:

- Charles Perceval & Caroline Perceval – 20 Nov 1820 (Marriage, **St. Peter Parish**)

Charles Perceval (husband):

    Residence - St. Peter Parish - November 20, 1820

Caroline Perceval (wife):

    Residence - St. Peter Parish - November 20, 1820

Wedding Witnesses:

Robert Perceval & John Graves

- Charles Perceval & Margaret Perceval

  - Lydia Elizabeth Perceval – bapt. 26 May 1754 (Baptism, **St. Audoen Parish**)

- Charles F. Perceval & Unknown

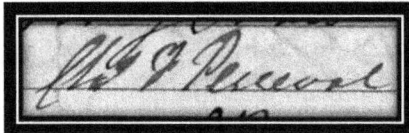

Signature:

Hurst

○ Caroline Perceval & Francis Patterson Studdert – 19 Jul 1849 (Marriage, **St. Peter Parish**)

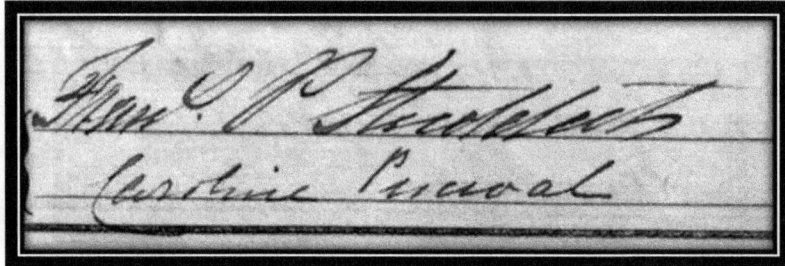

Signatures:

Caroline Perceval (daughter):

    Residence - 4 Mespill Parade - July 19, 1849

Francis Patterson Studdert, son of Richard Studdert (son-in-law):

    Residence - Little James Street - July 19, 1849

    Occupation - Clerk - July 19, 1849

Richard Studdert (father):

    Occupation - Clerk in Holy Orders

Charles F. Perceval (father):

    Occupation - Captain in the Army

Wedding Witnesses:

George Studdert & Robert E. Reeves

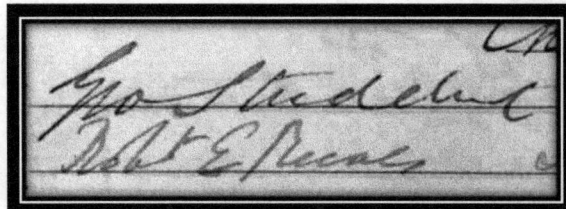

Signatures:

Perceval Surname Ireland: 1600s to 1900s

○ Charles William Perceval & Charlotte Alice Shaw – 28 Jul 1868 (Marriage, **St. Stephen Parish**)

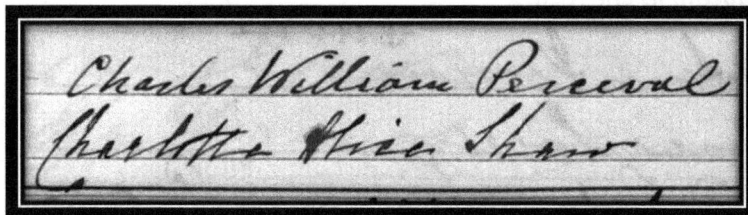

Signatures:

- Caroline Wilhelmina Perceval – b. 25 May 1870, bapt. 22 Jun 1870 (Baptism, **Leeson Park Parish**)
- Wilfred Shaw Perceval – b. 10 Jun 1883, bapt. 11 Jul 1883 (Baptism, **Leeson Park Parish**)

Charles William Perceval (son):

Residence - 5 Wilton Terrace - July 28, 1868

14 Lansdowne Road - June 22, 1870

36 Northumberland Road - July 11, 1883

Occupation - Esquire - July 28, 1868

Gentleman - July 11, 1883

Charlotte Alice Shaw, daughter of Henry Shaw (daughter-in-law):

Residence - 6 Wilton Terrace - July 28, 1868

Henry Shaw (father):

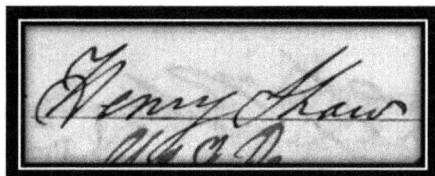

Signature:

Occupation - Captain in the Dublin City Artillery

Hurst

Charles F. Perceval (father):

Residence - Captain in the Army

Wedding Witnesses:

Henry Shaw & Charles F. Perceval

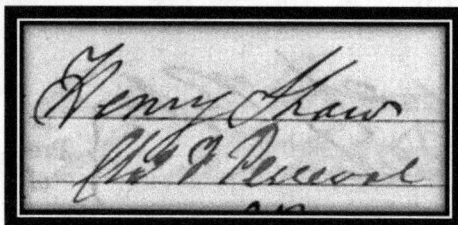

Signatures:

- David Perceval & Elizabeth Perceval

  o Elizabeth Perceval – bapt. 18 Jul 1695 (Baptism, **St. Michan Parish**)

  o Mary Perceval – bapt. 7 Feb 1697 (Baptism, **St. Mary Parish**)

  o Samuel Perceval – bapt. 3 Mar 1700 (Baptism, **St. Mary Parish**)

  o Martha Perceval – bapt. 27 Apr 1703 (Baptism, **St. Mary Parish**)

David Perceval (father):

Occupation - Weaver - July 18, 1695

February 7, 1697

March 3, 1700

April 27, 1703

- Edward Perceval & Margaret Perceval

  o Lydia Perceval – b. 20 Sep 1893, bapt. 25 Sep 1893 (Baptism, **Rotunda Chapel Parish**)

Perceval Surname Ireland: 1600s to 1900s

Edward Perceval (father):

Residence - 11 South King Street - September 25, 1893

Occupation - Carpenter - September 25, 1893

- Edward Perceval & Mary Perceval
  - William Perceval – bapt. 25 Mar 1699 (Baptism, **St. Michan Parish**)

Edward Perceval (father):

Residence - Laborer - March 25, 1699

- Francis Perceval & Mary Tobin
  - James Edward Perceval – b. 28 Feb 1886, bapt. 11 Mar 1886 (Baptism, **SS. Michael & John Parish** (RC))

Francis Perceval (father):

Residence - Ship Street Barracks - March 11, 1886

- George Perceval & Margaret Doyle
  - George Perceval – bapt. 1811 (Baptism, **St. Mary Parish** (RC))
- George Perceval & Mary Perceval
  - Catherine Perceval – bapt. 29 Jan 1668 (Baptism, **St. Michan Parish**)
  - Philip Perceval – bapt. 6 Aug 1670 (Baptism, **St. Michan Parish**)
  - William Perceval – bapt. 15 Dec 1671 (Baptism, **St. Michan Parish**)
  - Mary Perceval – bapt. 25 Mar 1673 (Baptism, **St. Michan Parish**), bur. 17 Feb 1674 (Burial, **St. Audoen Parish**)
  - Charles Perceval – bapt. 12 Feb 1674 (Baptism, **St. Michan Parish**)

Hurst

George Perceval (father):

Occupation - Esquire - January 29, 1668

August 6, 1670

December 15, 1671

March 25, 1673

February 12, 1674

- George Perceval & Unknown
  - Unknown Perceval (Child) – bur. 3 Dec 1797 (Burial, **St. Mary Parish**)

George Perceval (father):

Residence - Britain Street - December 3, 1797

- George Perceval & Unknown
  - William George Perceval & Elizabeth Rutledge – 1 Feb 1872 (Marriage, **Clontarf Parish**)

Signatures:

William George Perceval (son):

Residence - Sea View Bremoor Balbriggan, Balrothery Parish - February 1, 1872

Occupation - Contractor - February 1, 1872

Perceval Surname Ireland: 1600s to 1900s

Elizabeth Rutledge, daughter of John Rutledge (daughter-in-law):

Residence - 2 Casino Terrace, Clontarf - February 1, 1872

John Rutledge (father):

Occupation - Gentleman

George Perceval (father):

Occupation - Officer of Coast Guard

Wedding Witnesses:

John Rutledge & William Poole

Signatures:

- Gulielmo Perceval & Anne Unknown
    - Eleanor Perceval – b. 1749, bapt. 1749 (Baptism, **St. Andrew Parish** (RC))
    - Gulielmo Perceval – bapt. 1751 (Baptism, **St. Andrew Parish** (RC))
    - Robert Perceval – bapt. 1753 (Baptism, **St. Andrew Parish** (RC))
    - Anne Perceval – bapt. 1756 (Baptism, **St. Andrew Parish** (RC))
    - Catherine Perceval – bapt. 1761 (Baptism, **St. Andrew Parish** (RC))
- Humphrey Perceval & Elizabeth Unknown
    - John Perceval – bur. 15 Nov 1699 (Burial, **St. Michan Parish**)

Hurst

Humphrey Perceval (father):

Occupation - Soldier - November 15, 1699

- James Perceval & Anne Flood

  - Samuel Perceval – bapt. 1 Nov 1841 (Baptism, **St. James Parish (RC)**)

  - Anne Perceval – bapt. 8 Apr 1844 (Baptism, **St. James Parish (RC)**)

  - Michael Perceval – bapt. 4 Nov 1847 (Baptism, **St. James Parish (RC)**)

  - Francis Perceval – bapt. 20 May 1850 (Baptism, **St. James Parish (RC)**)

- James Perceval & Unknown

  - Martha Westby Perceval & Philips Newton – 14 Oct 1865 (Marriage, **St. Peter Parish**)

Signatures:

Martha Westby Perceval (daughter):

Residence - 29 York Street - October 14, 1865

Philips Newton, son of Hubert Newton (son-in-law):

Residence - Ballington Rath-, Co. Wicklow - October 14, 1865

Occupation - Esquire - October 14, 1865

Hubert Newton (father):

Occupation - Lieutenant in the Army & J. P. [Justice of the Peace]

James Perceval (father):

Occupation - Major in the Army

Wedding Witnesses:

Samuel Little & Raffe Owen

Signatures:

o   Mary Westby Perceval & Thomas Mooney – 28 Feb 1866 (Marriage, **St. Peter Parish**)

Signatures:

Mary Westby Perceval (daughter):

Residence - 29 York Street - February 28, 1866

Thomas Mooney, son of George Mooney (son-in-law):

Residence - Lenton, Nottingham - February 28, 1866

Hurst

Occupation - Clerk in Holy Orders - February 28, 1866

George Mooney (father):

Occupation - Schoolmaster

James Perceval (father):

Occupation - Major in the Army

Wedding Witnesses:

George Mooney & J. I. Perceval

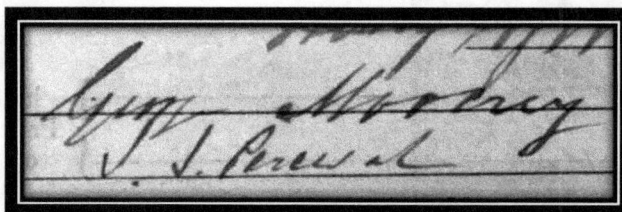

Signatures:

- James Archibold Perceval & Isabel Orson – 22 Sep 1831 (Marriage, St. Peter Parish)
  - Grace Mary Perceval – bapt. 6 Feb 1833 (Baptism, St. Mary Parish)
  - Susan Perceval – b. 10 Jul 1834, bapt. 19 Sep 1834 (Baptism, St. Peter Parish)
  - Mary Anne Burrowes Perceval – b. 18 Apr 1838, bapt. 15 Dec 1838 (Baptism, St. Mary Parish)
  - Henry Perceval – bapt. 7 May 1844 (Baptism, St. Catherine Parish (RC))

James Archibald Perceval (father):

Residence - 32 Charlemont Street, St. Peter Parish - September 22, 1831

23 Mary Street - February 6, 1833

Harold's Cross - September 19, 1834

25 Denmark Street - December 15, 1838

Perceval Surname Ireland: 1600s to 1900s

Occupation - Gentleman - February 6, 1833

Pawn Broker - December 15, 1838

Isabel Orson (mother):

Residence - Denmark Street - September 22, 1831

Occupation - Spinster - September 22, 1831

Wedding Witnesses:

J. James Orson & Elizabeth Miller

- John Perceval & Anne Maguire – 15 Jan 1839 (Marriage, **Rathmines Parish** (RC))

  o   William Perceval – b. 4 Jan 1842, bapt. 23 Jan 1842 (Baptism, **St. Matthew Parish**)

  o   Joseph Perceval – b. 13 Feb 1843, bapt. 13 Aug 1843 (Baptism, **St. Matthew Parish**) (Baptism, **St. Mary Parish** (RC))

  o   Mary Anne Perceval – bapt. 1847 (Baptism, **St. Mary Parish** (RC))

John Perceval (father):

Residence - Irishtown - January 23, 1842

August 13, 1843

Occupation - Watchmaker - January 23, 1842

August 13, 1843

Wedding Witnesses:

Martin B. Rattigan & Winifred Maguire

- John Perceval & Catherine Perceval

  o Anne Perceval – bapt. 16 Apr 1713 (Baptism, **St. Mary Parish**)

- John Perceval & Margaret Perceval

  o Jane Perceval – bapt. 15 Aug 1708 (Baptism, **St. John Parish**)

John Perceval (father):

Residence - Christ Church - August 15, 1708

Occupation - File Cutter - August 15, 1708

- John Perceval & Mary Perceval

  o Lionel Perceval – bapt. 3 Mar 1736 (Baptism, **St. Catherine Parish**)

- John Perceval & Mary Perceval

  o David Perceval – bapt. 17 Aug 1750 (Baptism, **St. Mark Parish**)

John Perceval (father):

Residence - At the Folly - August 17, 1750

- John Perceval & Mary Perceval

  o John Perceval – bapt. 2 Mar 1826 (Baptism, **St. Mary, Pro Cathedral Parish (RC)**)

John Perceval (father):

Residence - King Street - March 2, 1826

- John Perceval & Mary Anne Burrowes – 28 Oct 1809 (Marriage, **St. Mary Parish**)

John Perceval (husband):

Occupation - Esquire - October 28, 1809

Perceval Surname Ireland: 1600s to 1900s

- John Perceval & Rose Perceval

  o Duke Perceval – bapt. 20 Jan 1740 (Baptism, **St. Catherine Parish**)

- John Perceval & Unknown

  o Mary Perceval – bapt. 19 Nov 1680 (Baptism, **St. John Parish**)

- John Perceval & Unknown

  o John Perceval – bapt. 1 May 1684 (Baptism, **St. Michan Parish**)

John Perceval (father):

Occupation - Esquire - May 1, 1684

- John Perceval & Unknown

  o David Perceval – bur. 25 Feb 1751 (Burial, **St. Mark Parish**)

- John Perceval & Unknown

  o Joseph Perceval & Margaret McNight – 5 Apr 1875 (Marriage, **Kilmainham Parish**)

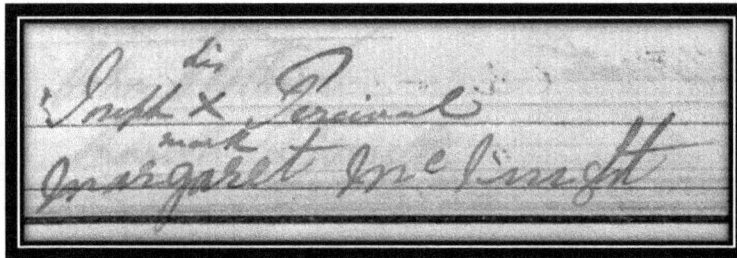

Signatures:

Joseph Perceval (son):

Residence - Richmond Barracks - April 5, 1875

Occupation - Soldier, Private, 29th Regiment - April 5, 1875

Margaret McNight, daughter of William McNight (daughter-in-law):

Residence - Richmond - April 5, 1875

15

William McNight (father):

    Occupation - Clerk & Sexton

John Perceval (father):

    Occupation - Carpenter

Wedding Witnesses:

John Jordan & Mary Dillon

Signatures:

- John Perceval & Unknown
  - Henry Perceval & Selina Moore Stephenson – 1 Sep 1891 (Marriage, **St. Thomas Parish**)

Signatures:

Perceval Surname Ireland: 1600s to 1900s

Henry Perceval (son):

   Residence - 68 Lower Gloucester Street - September 1, 1891

      Longford - September 1, 1891

   Occupation - Farmer - September 1, 1891

   Relationship Status at Marriage - widow

Selina Moore Stephenson, daughter of Henry Moore (daughter-in-law):

   Residence - 1 Herbert Avenue, Merrion, Co. Dublin - September 1, 1891

   Relationship Status at Marriage - widow

Henry Moore (father):

   Occupation - Merchant

John Perceval (father):

   Occupation - Farmer

Wedding Witnesses:

George W. Clarendon, Thomas P. Callaghan, & Mary D. Moore

Signatures:

Hurst

- John Caesar Thorndyke (T h o r n d y k e) Perceval & Caroline Louisa Unknown

  - Douglas Thorndyke (T h o r n d y k e) Perceval – b. 28 Dec 1892, bapt. 2 Dec 1900 (Baptism, **St. Stephen Parish**)

  - Harold John Thorndyke (T h o r n d y k e) Perceval – b. 11 Mar 1892, bapt. 2 Dec 1900 (Baptism, **St. Stephen Parish**)

  - Herbert Thorndyke (T h o r n d y k e) Perceval – b. 2 Nov 1894, bapt. 2 Dec 1900 (Baptism, **St. Stephen Parish**)

  - John Thorndyke (T h o r n d y k e) Perceval – b. 4 Nov 1897, bapt. 2 Dec 1900 (Baptism, **St. Stephen Parish**)

  - Mabel Evelyn Louise Perceval – b. 19 Jan 1900, bapt. 2 Dec 1900 (Baptism, **St. Stephen Parish**)

John Caesar Thorndyke Perceval (father):

Residence - 6 Ashfield Avenue, Ranelagh - December 2, 1900

Occupation - Surveyor - December 2, 1900

- Joseph Perceval & Ellen Sheehan – 20 Sep 1807 (Marriage, **Cork -South Parish (RC)**)

Ellen Sheehan (wife):

Residence - Terrace - September 20, 1807

Wedding Witnesses:

John Walsh & Mary Garvy

18

Perceval Surname Ireland: 1600s to 1900s

- Joseph Perceval & Hannah Huntington, bur. 22 Apr 1692 (Burial, **St. John Parish**) – 9 Nov 1676 (Marriage, **St. Michan Parish**)

  o Samuel Perceval – bapt. 19 Apr 1684 (Baptism, **St. John Parish**)

  o Benjamin Perceval – bapt. 12 Apr 1686 (Baptism, **St. John Parish**), bur. 24 Apr 1687 (Burial, **St. John Parish**)

  o Mary Perceval – bur. 12 Dec 1690 (Burial, **St. John Parish**)

- Joseph Perceval, bur. 14 Nov 1728 (Burial, **St. John Parish**) & Jane MacGin, bur. 2 Mar 1719 (Burial, **St. John Parish**) – 8 Nov 1692 (Marriage, **St. John Parish**)

- Kene Perceval & Mary Anne Unknown

  o William Perceval – bapt. 1 Jul 1752 (Baptism, **St. Mary Parish**)

Kene Perceval (father):

Occupation - Reverend - July 1, 1752

- Maxwell H. S. Perceval & Hyacinth Unknown

  o Maxwell O. Perceval – b. 14 Apr 1902, bapt. 12 May 1902 (Baptism, **Kenmare Parish**)

  o Maxwell G. H. Perceval – b. 24 May 1903, bapt. 23 Jun 1903 (Baptism, **Kenmare Parish**)

Maxwell H. S. Perceval (father):

Residence - Lansdowne Lodge - May 12, 1902

June 23, 1903

Occupation - Land Agent - May 12, 1902

Land Agent & J. P. [Justice of the Peace] **- June 23, 1903**

Hurst

- Michael Perceval & Anne Hand

  o Honor Perceval – bapt. 10 Dec 1834 (Baptism, **St. James Parish (RC)**)

- Michael Perceval & Mary Byrne (B y r n e) – 23 Oct 1848 (Marriage, **St. Andrew Parish (RC)**)

Wedding Witnesses:

Edward Byrne & Mary Cassidy

- Patrick Perceval & Mary Unknown

  o James Perceval & Helen Connor – 12 Feb 1905 (Marriage, **St. Mary, Haddington Road Parish (RC)**)

James Perceval (son):

Residence - Allenwood, Robertstown, Co. Kildare - February 12, 1905

Helen Connor, daughter of John Connor & Anne Unknown (daughter-in-law):

Residence - Allenwood, Co. Kildare - February 12, 1905

Wedding Witnesses:

Christopher O'Hara & Bridget Dunne

- Philip Perceval & Martha Donnellan – 10 Jun 1713 (Marriage, **St. Bride Parish**)

Philip Perceval (husband):

Occupation - Esquire - June 10, 1713

Perceval Surname Ireland: 1600s to 1900s

- Philip Perceval, bur. 17 Aug 1751 (Burial, **St. Audoen Parish**) & Martha Unknown, bur. 17 Aug 1751 (Burial, **St. Audoen Parish**)

Philip Perceval (Husband):

   Residence - England - before August 17, 1751

Martha Unknown (wife):

   Residence - England - before August 17, 1751

- Robert Perceval & Anne Brereton – 9 May 1795 (Marriage, **St. Anne Parish**)

Robert Perceval (husband):

   Occupation - Doctor - May 9, 1795

- Robert Perceval & Bridget Perceval
  - Charlotte Perceval – bapt. 5 Oct 1755 (Baptism, **St. Mary Parish**)
- Robert Perceval & Frances Armstrong – 3 Mar 1775 (Marriage, **St. Mary Parish**)

Robert Perceval (husband):

   Occupation - Esquire - March 3, 1775

- Robert Perceval & Jane Perceval
  - John Perceval – bapt. 9 Sep 1718 (Baptism, **St. Mary Parish**)
  - Robert Perceval – b. 23 Dec 1718, bapt. 23 Jan 1719 (Baptism, **St. Mary Parish**)
  - Martha Perceval – b. 13 Jul 1723, bapt. 11 Aug 1723 (Baptism, **St. Mary Parish**)
  - Mary Perceval – b. 1 Aug 1724, bapt. 1 Sep 1724 (Baptism, **St. Mary Parish**)
  - Edward Perceval – b. 20 Dec 1725, bapt. 28 Dec 1725 (Baptism, **St. Mary Parish**)

Hurst

Robert Perceval (father):

Occupation - Esquire - January 23, 1719

September 1, 1724

December 28, 1725

- Robert Perceval & Unknown

  o Edward Perceval – bapt. 12 Sep 1735 (Baptism, **St. Mary Parish**)

- Samuel Perceval & Elizabeth Perceval

  o Joseph Perceval – bapt. 25 Mar 1733 (Baptism, **St. Audoen Parish**)

- Samuel Perceval & Grace Unknown

  o Mary Perceval – bapt. 12 Jul 1757 (Baptism, **St. Catherine Parish**)

  o Hannah Perceval – bapt. 14 Jul 1760 (Baptism, **St. Catherine Parish**)

- Samuel Perceval & Unknown

  o Robert Perceval – bur. 2 Feb 1688 (Burial, **St. Nicholas Within Parish**)

- Thomas Perceval & Jane Perceval

  o John Perceval – bapt. 7 Mar 1760 (Baptism, **St. Mary Parish**)

- Thomas Perceval & Unknown

  o Frances Perceval & James Charles Price – 21 Sep 1892 (Marriage, **St. Peter Parish**)

Signatures:

Perceval Surname Ireland: 1600s to 1900s

Frances Perceval (daughter):

    Residence - Drumshaw Bo, Co. Leitrim - September 21, 1892

James Charles Price, son of James Price (son-in-law):

    Residence - 78 Heytesbury Street, Dublin - September 21, 1892

    Occupation - Ironmonger - September 21, 1892

James Price (father):

    Occupation - Farmer

Thomas Perceval (father):

    Occupation - Farmer

Wedding Witnesses:

William Pike & Robert Price

Signatures:

- Unknown Perceval & Margaret Unknown
  - William Hankins Perceval – bapt. 23 Dec 1808 (Baptism, **St. Mary, Pro Cathedral Parish (RC)**)
- Unknown Perceval & Sarah Corbett, bur. 5 May 1757 (Burial, **St. Patrick Parish**)

Unknown Perceval (husband):

    Occupation - Reverend, Doctor

Hurst

Sarah Corbett, daughter of Unknown Corbett (wife):

    Residence - St. Patrick Parish - May 5, 1757

    Place of Burial - St. Patrick's Church Cemetery - May 5, 1757

Unknown Corbett (father):

    Occupation - Deacon of St. Patrick's Church

- Unknown Perceval & Unknown
  - Unknown Perceval (Son) – bur. 29 Oct 1751 (Burial, **St. Mark Parish**)
- Unknown Perceval & Unknown
  - Unknown Perceval – bur. 6 Sep 1761 (Burial, **St. Audoen Parish**)

Unknown Perceval (son or daughter):

    Age at Death - child

Unknown Perceval (faher):

    Occupation - Captain - September 6, 1761

- Unknown Perceval & Unknown
  - Charles G. G. Perceval

Signature:

Perceval Surname Ireland: 1600s to 1900s

- Unknown Perceval & Unknown

  o J. Perceval

Signature:

- Vernon (V e r n o n) John Perceval & Frances Farmer (F a r m e r) – 20 Nov 1841 (Marriage, **St. Mark Parish**)

Signatures:

Vernon John Perceval (husband):

    Residence - St. Mark Parish - November 20, 1841

Frances Farmer (wife):

    Residence - St. Mary Parish - November 20, 1841

Wedding Witnesses:

Walter Farmer & Martha Robinson

Signatures:

- Walter Perceval & Mary Perceval

  o Eleanor Perceval – bapt. 21 Mar 1707 (Baptism, **St. Catherine Parish**)

  o Walter Perceval – bapt. 5 Jan 1711 (Baptism, **St. Catherine Parish**)

- Westby Perceval & Elizabeth Cannon – 14 Dec 1776 (Marriage, **St. Mary Parish**)

  o Leticia Mary Perceval – bapt. 25 Mar 1778 (Baptism, **St. Mary Parish**)

Westby Perceval (father):

Residence - Philipstown, Co. Meath - December 14, 1776

Occupation - Esquire - December 14, 1776

March 25, 1778

- Westby Perceval & Margaret Lysaght – 9 Aug 1817 (Marriage, **St. Peter Parish**)

Westby Perceval (husband):

Residence - St. Peter Parish - August 9, 1817

Margaret Lysaght (wife):

Residence - St. Peter Parish - August 9, 1817

Wedding Witnesses:

Thomas Lysaght & David Lysaght

- William Perceval & Anne Perceval

  o William Perceval – b. 14 Feb 1816, bapt. 27 Feb 1816 (Baptism, **St. George Parish**)

  o Caroline Perceval – b. 30 Apr 1818, bapt. 13 May 1818 (Baptism, **St. Peter Parish**)

  o Richard Perceval – b. 24 Dec 1819, bapt. 10 Jan 1820 (Baptism, **St. Peter Parish**)

Perceval Surname Ireland: 1600s to 1900s

- William Perceval & Elizabeth Smith – 8 Dec 1774 (Marriage, **St. Peter Parish**)

- William Perceval & Elizabeth Unknown

  o Anne Perceval – bapt. 4 Jul 1756 (Baptism, **St. Catherine Parish**)

- William Perceval & Mary Perceval

  o Robert Perceval – bapt. 20 May 1829 (Baptism, **St. Mary Parish**)

William Perceval (father):

Residence - No. 90 Dorset Street - May 20, 1829

Occupation - Private - May 20, 1829

- William Perceval & Mary Thompson – 29 May 1828 (Marriage, **St. George Parish**)

Signatures:

  o William Perceval – b. 11 Nov 1830, bapt. 15 Dec 1830 (Baptism, **St. George Parish**)

William Perceval (father):

Residence - Knight's Brook, Co. Meath - May 29, 1828

December 15, 1830

Occupation - Gentleman - December 15, 1830

Mary Thompson (mother):

Residence - St. George Parish - May 29, 1828

Hurst

Wedding Witnesses:

John Thompson & John Doran

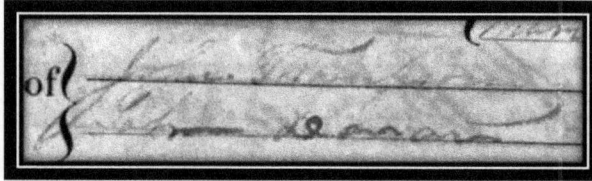

Signatures:

* William Perceval & Unknown
  * Henry Perceval & Harriet Echlin – 1 May 1850 (Marriage, **St. Peter Parish**)

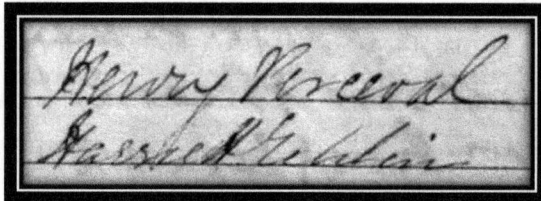

Signatures:

Henry Perceval (son):

    Residence - 32 South Frederick Street, St. Anne Parish - May 1, 1850

    Occupation - Esquire - May 1, 1850

Harriet Echlin, daughter of John Echlin (daughter-in-law):

    Residence - 9 Heytesbury Terrace, St. Peter Parish - May 1, 1850

John Echlin (father):

    Occupation - Esquire

William Perceval (father):

    Occupation - Captain in Army

Perceval Surname Ireland: 1600s to 1900s

Wedding Witnesses:

William Echlin & Edmund John Armstrong

Signatures:

o Alice F. Perceval & Robert Kearney (K e a r n e y) – 30 Nov 1855 (Marriage, **St. Bride Parish**)

Signatures:

Alice Perceval (daughter):

Residence - Newport, Tipperary - November 30, 1855

Robert Kearney, son of Robert Kearney (son-in-law):

Residence - Ship Street Barracks - November 30, 1855

Occupation - Ensign, 97th Regiment - November 30, 1855

Robert Kearney (father):

Occupation - Gentleman

William Perceval (father):

Occupation - Colonel in the Army

Hurst

Wedding Witnesses:

Samuel Evans Bradshaw & Mary J. Bradshaw

Signatures:

- William Perceval & Unknown
  - Alice Perceval & Theophilus Little – 27 Feb 1872 (Marriage, **Clontarf Parish**)

Signatures:

Alice Perceval (daughter):

Residence - Strandville, Clontarf, Co. Dublin - February 27, 1872

Theophilus Little, son of John Theophilus Little (son-in-law):

Residence - Dunningstown Park, St. Canice Park, Kilkenny - February 27, 1872

Occupation - Esquire - February 27, 1872

John Theophilus Little (father):

Occupation - Esquire

Perceval Surname Ireland: 1600s to 1900s

William Perceval (father):

Occupation - Esquire

Wedding Witnesses:

Thomas Jones & William Perceval

Signatures:

o William Perceval & Anne Clarke – 27 Jan 1874 (Marriage, **St. George Parish**)

Signatures:

▪ William John Perceval – b. 16 Feb 1875, bapt. 9 May 1875 (Baptism, **Clontarf Parish**)

William Perceval (son):

Residence - Strand Villa, Clontarf - January 27, 1874

Clontarf - May 9, 1875

Occupation - Jeweler - January 27, 1874

Gentleman - May 9, 1875

Hurst

Anne Clarke, daughter of John Robert Clarke (daughter-in-law):

    Residence - 15th Street Richmond Street - January 27, 1874

John Robert Clarke (father):

    Occupation - Esquire

William Perceval (father):

    Occupation - Esquire

Wedding Witnesses:

John Robert Clarke & John G. McEntagart

Signatures:

Individual Baptisms/Births

None Were Listed

Individual Burials

- Anne Perceval – b. 1741, d. 23 Jun 1824, bur. 1824 (Burial, **St. Peter Parish**)

Anne Perceval (deceased):

   Residence - Molesworth Street - June 23, 1824

   Age at Death - 83 years

- Anne Perceval – b. 1763, bur. 16 Nov 1833 (Burial, **St. Audoen Parish**)

Anne Perceval (deceased):

   Residence - Back Lane - before November 16, 1833

   Age at Death - 70 years

- Bridget Perceval – b. 1761, bur. 5 May 1827 (Burial, **St. Audoen Parish**)

Bridget Perceval (deceased):

   Residence - St. Audoen Parish - before May 5, 1827

   Age at Death - 66 years

- Caroline Perceval – bur. 4 Jun 1805 (Burial, **St. Paul Parish**)

- Catherine Perceval – bur. 6 Jan 1681 (Burial, **St. Audoen Parish**)

- Daniel Perceval – bur. 5 Oct 1761 (Burial, **St. Paul Parish**)

- Dominick Perceval – bur. 22 May 1626 (Burial, **St. John Parish**)

- Edward Perceval – bur. 5 Feb 1685 (Burial, **St. John Parish**)

Perceval Surname Ireland: 1600s to 1900s

- Elizabeth Perceval – bur. 12 Nov 1755 (Burial, **St. Paul Parish**)

- Elizabeth Perceval – bur. 18 Jun 1813 (Burial, **St. Mark Parish**)

Elizabeth Perceval (deceased):

Residence - Townsend Street - before June 18, 1813

- Elizabeth Perceval – b. 1781, bur. 6 Dec 1831 (Burial, **St. Mark Parish**)

Elizabeth Perceval (deceased):

Residence - Townsend Street - before December 6, 1831

Age at Death - 50 years

- Frances Perceval – bur. 18 Feb 1637 (Burial, **St. John Parish**)

- Francis Perceval – bur. 10 May 1637 (Burial, **St. John Parish**)

- George Perceval – bur. 25 Jul 1776 (Burial, **St. Paul Parish**)

- George Perceval – bur. 22 May 1814 (Burial, **St. Mary Parish**)

George Perceval (deceased):

Residence - Dorset Street - before May 22, 1814

- Hannah Perceval – bur. 17 Feb 1748 (Burial, **St. Audoen Parish**)

- James Perceval – bur. 30 May 1809 (Burial, **St. Paul Parish**)

- James A. Perceval – b. 1806, bur. 6 Feb 1841 (Burial, **St. Peter Parish**)

James A. Perceval (deceased):

Residence - Talbot Street - before February 6, 1841

Age at Death - 35 years

Hurst

- John Perceval – bur. 26 Feb 1723 (Burial, **St. Nicholas Without Parish**)

John Perceval (deceased):

    Residence - Han Lane - before February 26, 1723

- John Perceval – b. 1808, bur. 30 May 1834 (Burial, **St. Catherine Parish**)

John Perceval (deceased):

    Residence - Harold's Cross - before May 30, 1834

    Age at Death - 26 years

    Cause of Death - fever

- Margaret Perceval – b. 1778, bur. 3 Mar 1862 (Burial, **St. Peter Parish**)

Margaret Perceval (deceased):

    Residence - 129 Lower Baggot Street - before March 3, 1862

    Age at Death - 84 years

- Martha S. Perceval – b. Nov 1827, bur. 19 Apr 1828 (Burial, **St. Mary Parish**)

Martha S. Perceval (deceased):

    Residence - Seville Place - before April 19, 1828

    Age at Death - 2 ½ years

- Mary Perceval – bur. 23 Dec 1807 (Burial, **St. Peter Parish**)

Mary Perceval (deceased):

    Residence - King Street - before December 23, 1807

Perceval Surname Ireland: 1600s to 1900s

- Mary Perceval – b. 1807, bur. 21 Jul 1833 (Burial, **St. Nicholas Without Parish**)

Mary Perceval (deceased):

    Residence - Stephen's Green - before July 21, 1833

    Age at Death - 26 years

- Mary Anne Perceval – b. 1839, bur. 12 Apr 1841 (Burial, **St. Peter Parish**)

Mary Anne Perceval (deceased):

    Residence - Stephen Street - before April 12, 1841

    Age at Death - 2 years

    Place of Burial - St. Kevin's Cemetery

- Mary Anne Perceval – b. 1787, bur. 16 Nov 1855 (Burial, **St. Peter Parish**)

Mary Anne Perceval (deceased):

    Residence - 5 Digges Street - before November 16, 1855

    Age at Death - 68 years

- Philip Perceval – bur. 13 Jun 1718 (Burial, **St. Audoen Parish**)

Philip Perceval (deceased):

    Age at Death - child

- Rose Perceval – bur. 29 Jan 1744 (Burial, **St. Paul Parish**)

Hurst

- Unknown Perceval (Child) – bur. 28 Oct 1799 (Burial, St. Mary Parish)

Unknown Perceval (Child) (deceased):

   Residence - Stephen's Green - October 28, 1799

- Unknown Perceval (Mr.) – bur. 10 Apr 1787 (Burial, St. Mary Parish)
- Unknown Perceval (Mr.) – bur. 15 Feb 1806 (Burial, St. Mary Parish)

Unknown Perceval (Mr.) (deceased):

   Residence - Liffey Street - before February 15, 1806

- Unknown Perceval (Mrs.) – bur. 10 Jun 1745 (Burial, St. Mary Parish)
- Unknown Perceval (Mrs.) – bur. 12 Nov 1770 (Burial, St. Audoen Parish)

Unknown Perceval (Mrs.) (deceased):

   Residence - Digges Street - before November 12, 1770

- Unknown Perceval (Mrs.) – bur. 18 May 1777 (Burial, St. Mary Parish)

Unknown Perceval (Mrs.) (deceased):

   Residence - Stafford Street - before May 18, 1777

- Unknown Perceval (Mrs.) – bur. 3 Jul 1779 (Burial, St. Mary Parish)

Unknown Perceval (Mrs.) (deceased):

   Residence - Miltown Road - before July 3, 1779

Perceval Surname Ireland: 1600s to 1900s

- Westby Perceval – b. 1772, bur. 20 Nov 1835 (Burial, **St. Peter Parish**)

Westby Perceval (deceased):

    Residence - Baggot Street - before November 20, 1835

    Age at Death - 63 years

    Place of Burial - St. Peter Cemetery

- William Perceval – bur. 7 Mar 1804 (Burial, **St. Paul Parish**)
- William Perceval – bur. 12 Nov 1808 (Burial, **St. James Parish**)

William Perceval (deceased):

    Residence - Meath Street - before November 12, 1808

- William Perceval – b. 1763, bur. 6 Nov 1833 (Burial, **Killehsin Parish**)

William Perceval (deceased):

    Residence - Graigue - before November 6, 1833

    Age at Death - 70 years

Individual Marriages

- Anne Perceval & Marlborough Farrell – 12 Oct 1840 (Marriage, **St. Mary Parish**)

Signatures:

Anne Perceval (wife):

Residence - Akrlow, Co. Wicklow - October 12, 1840

Marlborough Farrell (husband):

Residence - St. Mary Parish - October 12, 1840

Wedding Witnesses:

William B. Perceval & George Baker

Signatures:

- Anne Perceval & Michael Murphy – 6 Dec 1782 (Marriage, **St. Michan Parish (RC)**)

  - Mary Murphy – bapt. 25 Aug 1785 (Baptism, **St. Michan Parish (RC)**)

- Anne Perceval & Patrick Andrews – 26 Nov 1724 (Marriage, **St. Anne Parish**)

Perceval Surname Ireland: 1600s to 1900s

- Anne Perceval & Thomas Cullen – 9 Nov 1842 (Marriage, **St. Mary, Pro Cathedral Parish (RC)**)

Wedding Witnesses:

Charles Kenahan & Mary Kenahan

- Anne Perceval & Thomas Mahony

  o   Elizabeth Mahony – bapt. 6 Apr 1803 (Baptism, **Cork -South Parish (RC)**)

- Anne Bridget Perceval & William Keating Clay – 1 May 1834 (Marriage, **St. Peter Parish**)

Anne Bridget Perceval (wife):

   Residence - Charlemont Street - May 1, 1834

William Keating Clay (husband):

   Residence - Wentworth Place - May 1, 1834

Wedding Witnesses:

J. B. Pounds & Elizabeth Hailey

- Catherine Perceval & Brewster Laughlin – 22 Oct 1737 (Marriage, **St. Michan Parish**)

Brewster Laughlin (husband):

   Occupation - Esquire - October 22, 1737

- Charlotte Perceval & James Farrell – 13 Jul 1799 (Marriage, **St. Mary Parish**)

- Elizabeth Perceval & James Madole – 1 Aug 1811 (Marriage, **St. Werburgh Parish**)

- Elizabeth Perceval & Patrick Drake – 22 Jun 1744 (Marriage, **St. Andrew Parish (RC)**)

Wedding Witnesses:

James Murphy & Jane Hagarty

Hurst

- Elizabeth Perceval & Patrick Toole

  - Robert Toole – bapt. Apr 1780 (Baptism, **St. Nicholas Parish (RC)**)

  - Patrick Toole – bapt. Mar 1783 (Baptism, **St. Nicholas Parish (RC)**)

- Emily Perceval & Thomas Palmer – 18 Mar 1837 (Marriage, **St. Peter Parish**)

Emily Perceval (wife):

Residence - **128 Baggot Street** - March 18, 1837

Occupation - **Spinster** - March 18, 1837

Thomas Palmer (husband):

Residence - **Summerhill, Co. Mayo** - March 18, 1837

Molesworth Street - March 18, 1837

Wedding Witnesses:

John Vincent & Richard Lysaght

- Hannah Perceval & Robert Barns (B a r n s) – 29 Sep 1786 (Marriage, **St. Catherine Parish (RC)**)

Wedding Witnesses:

Grace McMahon & Mary Barns

- Jane Perceval & Arthur French – Feb 1723 (Marriage, **St. Mary Parish**)

Arthur French (husband):

Occupation - **Esquire** - February 1723

Perceval Surname Ireland: 1600s to 1900s

- Jane Perceval & Henry Corbett Singleton

  - John Singleton – b. 1834, bapt. 1834 (Baptism, **St. Peter Parish**)

Henry Coobet Lingleton (father):

Residence - Adare, Co. Meath - 1834

- Jane Perceval & John Cooper – 18 Oct 1708 (Marriage, **St. Michan Parish**)

John Cooper (husband):

Occupation - Gentleman - October 18, 1708

- Margaret Perceval & Unknown Roache – 21 Mar 1760 (Marriage, **St. Paul Parish**)

- Mary Anne Perceval & Thomas Orr

  - Thomas Orr – b. 1869, bapt. 1869 (Baptism, **St. Mary Parish** (RC))

- Sarah Perceval & Samuel Lavis

  - Samuel Lavis – bapt. 31 Dec 1843 (Baptism, **Cork -SS. Peter & Paul Parish** (RC))

  - Elizabeth Lavis – bapt. 26 Apr 1846 (Baptism, **Cork -SS. Peter & Paul Parish** (RC))

- Winifred Perceval & Gulielmo Walsh

  - Winifred Anne Walsh – b. 9 Oct 1878, bapt. 10 Oct 1878 (Baptism, **St. Mary, Haddington Road Parish** (RC))

  - Gulielmo Walsh – b. 8 Aug 1881, bapt. 13 Aug 1881 (Baptism, **St. Mary, Haddington Road Parish** (RC))

  - Anne Mary Walsh – b. 25 Mar 1887, bapt. 28 Mar 1887 (Baptism, **St. Mary, Haddington Road Parish** (RC))

Hurst

Gulielmo Walsh (father):

Residence - 16 Haddington Road - October 10, 1878

August 13, 1881

March 28, 1887

- Winifred Perceval & William Walsh – 6 Jan 1867 (Marriage, **St. Mary Parish (RC)**)

Wedding Witnesses:

John Ruddock & Margaret Orr

Perceval Surname Ireland: 1600s to 1900s

Name Variations

Includes Latin and Abbreviated forms of names found in the original documents.

Abigail = Abigale, Abigall

Anne = Ann, Anna, Annae

Bartholomew = Barth, Bartholmeus, Bartholomeo

Bridget = Birgis, Brigid, Brigida, Bridgit

Catherine = Catharine, Catharina, Catharinae, Catherina, Cath, Catha, Cathae, Cathe, Cathn, Kate

Charles = Carolus, Charls, Chas

Christopher = Christoph

Daniel = Danielem, Danielis

Edmund = Edmond

Edward = Ed, Edwd

Eleanor = Eleo, Eleonora, Elinor, Ellenor

Elizabeth = Betty, Elisa, Elisabeth, Eliz, Eliza, Elizab, Elizh, Elizth

Ellen = Elena, Ellena

Emily = Emilia

Esther = Essie, Ester

Francis = Fransicum

George = Geo, Georg, Georgius

Grace = Gratiae

Gulielmo = Guil, Guillelmi, Gulielmum, Guillelmus, Gulmi

Helen = Helena

Perceval Surname Ireland: 1600s to 1900s

Honor = Hanora, Honora

James = Jacobi, Jacobus, Jas

Jane = Joanna

Jeanne = Jeannae, Joannae

Joan = Johanna, Joney

John = Jno, Joannem, Joannes, Johannis

Joseph = Jos

Juliana = Julian

Leticia = Letitia, Lettice, Letticia

Lewis = Louis

Luke = Lucas

Margaret = Margarita, Margaritae, Margeret, Marget, Margt

Martha = Marthae

Mary = Maria, My

Mary Anne = Marianna, Marianne, Maryanne

Michael = Michaelis, Michl

Patrick = Pat, Patt, Patk, Patricii, Patricius

Peter = Petri

Richard = Ricardi, Ricardus, Rich, Richd

Robert = Roberti

Rose = Rosa, Rosae

Thomas = Thom, Thomae, Thoms, Thos, Ths

Timothy = Timotheus, Timy

William = Wil, Will, Willm, Wm

Notes

Notes

Notes

Notes

Notes

Notes

Index

Perceval Surname Ireland: 1600s to 1900s

French
Arthur 42

H

Hand
Anne 20
Huntington
Burials
Hannah
1692 Apr 22 19
Hutchinson
Elizabeth 1
John 1

K

Kearney
Robert 29

L

L'Estrange
Collin 1
Jane 1
Spouses
Grace 1
Laughlin
Brewster 41
Lavis
Baptisms
Elizabeth
1846 Apr 26 43
Samuel
1843 Dec 31 43
Samuel 43
Little
John Theophilus 30

Theophilus 30
Lysaght
Margaret 26

M

MacGin
Burials
Jane
1719 Mar 2 19
Madole
James 41
Maguire
Anne 13
Mahony
Baptisms
Elizabeth
1803 Apr 6 41
Thomas 41
McNight
Margaret 15
William 15
Mooney
George 11
Thomas 11
Moore
Henry 17
Murphy
Baptisms
Mary
1785 Aug 25 40
Michael 40

N

Newton
Hubert 10
Philips 10

55

O

Hurst

Perceval Surname Ireland: 1600s to 1900s

Hurst

63

About The Author

Donovan Hurst graduated from San Diego State University with a Bachelor of Arts in the major field of studies of History and a minor in the field of studies of Anthropology. He is a current member of The General Society of Mayflower Descendants and has been conducting genealogical research for over 10 years tracing back his ancestors to their ancestral homelands in Denmark, England, France, Germany, Ireland, Norway, and Scotland.

www.ingramcontent.com/pod-product-compliance
Lightning Source LLC
Chambersburg PA
CBHW081200270326
41930CB00014B/3239